PARTICIPANT'S GUIDE

# WURMBRAND

## A SIX-SESSION STUDY ON THE COMPLETE TORTURED FOR CHRIST STORY

## the voice of the martyrs

DAVID **C** COOK

*transforming lives together*

WURMBRAND PARTICIPANT'S GUIDE
Published by David C Cook
4050 Lee Vance Drive
Colorado Springs, CO 80918 U.S.A.

Integrity Music Limited, a Division of David C Cook
Eastbourne, East Sussex BN23 6NT, England

The graphic circle C logo is a registered trademark of David C Cook.

Unless otherwise noted, all Scripture quotations are taken from the ESV® Bible
(The Holy Bible, English Standard Version®), copyright © 2001 by Crossway, a
publishing ministry of Good News Publishers. Used by permission. All rights
reserved. Scripture quotations marked NIV are taken from THE HOLY BIBLE,
NEW INTERNATIONAL VERSION®, NIV® Copyright © 1973, 1978, 1984,
2011 by Biblica, Inc.® Used by permission. All rights reserved worldwide.

ISBN 978-0-8307-7602-3
eISBN 978-0-8307-7628-3

The David C Cook Team: Wendi Lord, Rachael Stevenson, Susan Murdock
The Voice of the Martyrs Team: Cole Richards, Todd
Nettleton, Cheryl Odden, Olive Swan
Cover Design: Amy Konyndyk
Cover Photo: The Voice of the Martyrs, Inc.
Writers: Amanda and Stephen Sorenson

Printed in the United States of America
First Edition 2018

1 2 3 4 5 6 7 8 9 10

062818

# CONTENTS

# Unpacking the Message of Tortured for Christ

Richard and Sabina Wurmbrand's story is a truly inspiring account of lives lived faithfully for Christ under the real and ever-present threat of frightening and dangerous circumstances. Theirs is a story of amazing courage, heart-wrenching suffering, and mind-boggling love. It is a story of Christian faith lived out in bold action.

It is easy to label the Wurmbrands' story, as well as the stories of other faithful believers from the early apostles to modern-day Christians who suffer under relentless persecution, as demonstrations of exemplary faith—which, of course, they are. We often label the participants in these stories as heroes—people who faced the impossible and overachieved—and they are heroes, indeed.

Yet in the process of valuing and honoring these shining examples of biblical discipleship, we may mistakenly think of them as being in some mysterious way "supernatural" or exceptionally blessed and gifted to assume the roles God made available to them.

To a certain extent this is true. Such stories cannot occur without the enabling power of God's Spirit at work in the lives of the faithful. However, we must realize that this level of Spirit-led living is within the reach of every follower of Jesus! No matter how many labels of respect, honor, and admiration we put on the Wurmbrands and their story, it did not unfold in a vacuum.

The Wurmbrands were ordinary people—just like us—who at first pursued the world's idea of the good life and enjoyed all it had to offer. Their transformation to becoming people of faith who willingly endured great sacrifices of faith began as a seed that was prayerfully and faithfully kept until it was planted in the right place at the right time by the testimony of one, aged Christian man. That newfound faith grew into a powerful influence for good as it was deliberately rooted in and nurtured by the Word of God; developed a deep, abiding trust in God that overpowered the fear of whatever the Enemy might do and brought peace where the Enemy brought chaos; and yielded Christlike action made possible through the faithful support of a community of like-minded believers.

Under the fire of fierce persecution, the Wurmbrands' faith forced them to make pivotal choices based on a biblical understanding of what is most important in life and their unshakable commitment to expend their lives and resources on what truly matters.

Through this guide, we will explore how all of these threads fed into the tapestry of the Wurmbrands' story of ordinary followers of Jesus who made a powerful impact for God's kingdom while facing brutally painful and seemingly impossible circumstances. So please join with us and consider how God transforms ordinary people like us into faithful warriors for his kingdom who bring the message and hope of God's love into the darkest places. Learn and grow with us as we seek to build up our own faith so that we too will stand for Christ and have a life-changing impact on our world.

# 1

# WHO WILL STAND FOR CHRIST?

*The Communist Party launched a full-scale campaign against religion in Romania. Until this point, Richard's life as a pastor had been full of satisfaction. His salary could support Sabina and Mihai, and his church family loved and trusted him. But Richard wasn't at peace. Why had God allowed him to live as usual while a tyrannical dictatorship was destroying everything around him and while other Christians were suffering for their faith? Many nights Richard and Sabina prayed for God to give them a cross to bear. Soon their prayers would be answered.*

The Voice of the Martyrs, *Wurmbrand*

# Session Start-Up

## Let's Talk about That One

Do you know of any Christians who have been so concerned by their own comfort that while their brothers and sisters in Christ were suffering they prayed for God to give them a cross to bear?

What feelings or questions does a prayer like theirs cause you to consider?

Can you picture yourself praying like that? Why or why not?

## Let's Pray Together

*Dear Lord, your Word says your ways are not our ways and your thoughts are not our thoughts. For most of us, eagerly and joyfully bearing a cross in life—a cross that brings us to share in the sufferings of Jesus—is one of those thoughts we don't readily understand. Yes, in our minds we know that bearing the cross of Christ is a privilege, but when it comes to hardship, pain, and suffering, we'd rather avoid it. Forgive us for our lack of faith and trust in you. Be patient with us as we begin this study to learn more of your thoughts and ways. Strengthen and empower us as we seek to obey and do all you have commanded us to do. In the precious name of Jesus our Savior we pray. Amen.*

# Video Exploration

## Video Notes

- Christ first every day
- Richard Wurmbrand lives the good life
- At last! God answers the prayer of an ordinary carpenter
- The power of one faithful follower of Jesus
- The impact of Russia's "peaceful" invasion
- A question of loyalty
- Richard and Sabina make a pivotal choice
- How one makes such a costly choice
- Will you be ready?

## Video Discussion

1. It is not uncommon for followers of Jesus to talk about "standing for Christ" or "taking up our cross." When we say these words or hear them spoken by others, which images and thoughts come to mind, and what do those words mean to you?

In what ways might your understanding of taking up one's cross and standing for Christ differ from Richard and Sabina's understanding, or differ from the understanding of persecuted Christians today who live in places like China, Nigeria, or Iran?

As you think about these differences in experience and understanding, what action(s) do they prompt you to take as you go through daily life?

2. For many years, Christian Wölfkes prayed faithfully for the one thing he longed to accomplish with his life: to lead a Jew to Christ. How important do we tend to think one, single act of obedience done for God's kingdom really is, and how might that affect the way we view taking a stand for Christ?

In what ways does the role Wölfkes played in Wurmbrand's story change your thinking about who God calls and how he can enable each and every one of us to become witnesses who make a powerful impact for him in the world?

3. Our world is plagued with chaos and turmoil—evident in the abundance of lies, half-truths, misrepresentations, conflict, deception, manipulation, extortion, repression, grasping for power, oppression, and destruction of whatever is pure, good, and honoring to God. For Richard and Sabina, that chaos unfolded first during the Nazi occupation of Romania and then became far worse during Russia's takeover after World War II. The Russian agenda was to silence the influence of God's people in the culture, and there was no limit to the brutality and cruelty they would inflict to achieve their objective. How would you describe the Wurmbrands' understanding of the importance of standing up to speak the love and truth of Christ at that time?

What were you thinking as you watched Richard and Sabina assess what was happening during the Congress of the Cults and face that pivotal moment when Sabina challenged Richard to speak?

4. We know the cost the Wurmbrands (and many others) paid to stand for Christ at that time in Romania. What do you see as the pivotal choices and cost of standing for Christ in the culture in which we live?

# Growing into a More Biblical Faith Perspective

## Our Study Together

Significant benefits come our way when we live a life of faith in Jesus Christ. It is a relief, for example, to live in the peace and joy of knowing we have been forgiven and God's love for us can never be shaken. When we respond to God's calling on our lives and obediently love him with all our heart, soul, and strength, we can be confident we are living for a purpose that matters not only during our life in this world but for all eternity. And we can delight in the blessings of every good and perfect gift God sees fit to shower upon us.

But there are times when following Christ doesn't seem quite so beneficial—at least not in the ways we like to think of it. Life in obedience to Christ can be scary, dangerous, and very hard.

Richard and Sabina certainly experienced the benefits of a worldly idea of a "good life" on earth. Before he was introduced to Christ, Richard was a successful stockbroker. Charming and wealthy enough to indulge in any pleasures money could buy, he definitely had earned his playboy reputation. Sabina, raised in an Orthodox Jewish home, was a student at the Sorbonne when she met Richard. Free from her family's religious constraints, she enjoyed the carefree and unrestricted social pleasures of Paris and had big dreams for what she would accomplish in life.

But the faithful witness of an old Romanian carpenter who prayed to win just one of God's children for Christ revealed to the

Wurmbrands a goodness they had always longed for but could never quite acquire, no matter how hard they tried. When Richard, and later, Sabina, accepted Christ as Savior and Lord, their lives were transformed beyond what they could have imagined. Instead of indulging in the pleasures of the here and now, they discovered a very different "good life" in which they focused their desires and affections on eternity and serving Jesus who had forgiven their sins. Let's look deeper into what God's Word teaches us about the sacrifices of the truly good life of a disciple who is truly committed to Christ.

1. When we come into a relationship with Jesus, what does God's Word say we are (2 Cor. 5:17)?

It is clear that we aren't what we used to be, but what are we to become and do? Each of the following passages gives us a piece of the picture. Read each one and discuss what you discover about the life priorities of a disciple of Jesus.

- 1 John 2:1–6
- 2 Corinthians 5:18–20
- Luke 9:23–25
- Romans 12:1–2
- Philippians 1:27–29

2. The more we study the Bible and what it means to know the love of God, to be a "living sacrifice," to live in a "manner worthy of Christ," and to "take up the cross daily," the more we realize that the life of faith is not about us. It is, quite simply, all about God. What did Jesus teach about what a life lived for him would be like (Matt. 10:17–20, 22; Mark 13:9–11; Luke 21:12–15)?

In what ways did the lives of the apostles demonstrate that they understood what it meant to die to themselves and no longer live for their desires and comfort but for God and his purposes (Acts 5:17–22, 25–32; 21:10–13; 28:16–20, 23, 30–31)?          .

3. In one of his many books, Richard Wurmbrand wrote about a foundational perspective that helps us understand how he and Sabina could make the painfully difficult choices they made in order to stand for Christ. "The believer places himself before God like a canvas awaiting a painter. Obedience is taken for granted. The canvas, after all, does not resist the gentle pressure of the artist's brush. The Christian life is not a life of constant choices between the ways of Christ and those of the world. We are living His life. The choice has already been made; we have died to self."[1]

Paul told us, "I have been crucified with Christ. It is no longer I who live, but Christ lives in me" (Gal. 2:20). How many times have we heard, or even recited, this verse and never quite understood it this way?

Which choices—whether in lifestyle or relationships as well as in our spoken witness of Christ to the world around us—do we find difficult to make?

In what ways does our perception of these choices change if we truly believe we have died to self and the only choice is to speak the words and take the action that Jesus would?

How different are the choices of Jesus in contrast to the choices of our self-preserving and self-promoting selves?

4. Salvation is God's free gift to everyone who comes to him. But sin is also costly, and our salvation, our deliverance from sin, was purchased for us at a great price: the sacrificial blood of Jesus.

Richard and Sabina became keenly aware that anyone who chooses to be identified with Christ in this world—and obeys his mandate to live for him—will pay a price, and they were willing to pay it. The question we each must answer is whether we have counted the cost and decided that standing for Christ is worth everything.

In Philippians 3:7–10, Paul explained his understanding of gains and losses when it comes to our relationship with Christ. In what ways does his explanation help you to consider how much you value your relationship with Christ in contrast to the price that following him could cost?

Jesus once told a parable about the importance of counting the cost. Read Luke 14:25–33 and discuss the importance of counting the cost in light of our witness to the world of the love of Christ. Imagine, for example, if Richard and Sabina had not counted the cost and failed to stand firm. Imagine the torment of ridicule their torturers would have heaped upon them. Imagine the damage to the reputation of Christ's salvation. What do you see as the consequences of counting, or not counting, the cost of standing firm for Christ in your life?

5. Once we make the essential choice to take up the cross and follow wherever Jesus leads, our labor of faithfulness to his calling begins in earnest. It is important that we not only count the cost of faithfulness but prepare ourselves for what lies ahead. The apostle Peter understood the mission to which God has called every follower of Jesus. He wrote, "But you are a chosen race, a royal priesthood, a holy nation, a people for his own possession, that you may proclaim the excellencies of him who called you out of darkness into his marvelous light" (1 Pet. 2:9). He also understood the scope of the rewards and opposition every follower of Jesus could encounter.

Read 1 Peter 3:13–16 carefully and make a list of the perspectives and practices that can prepare our hearts and minds to face whatever opposition may come our way.

What else has God provided to help us live for his purposes and glory (2 Pet. 1:3–4)?

## Make It Personal

It is easy for the embarrassment of ridicule, the hardship of financial loss, or the fear of pain to shame us into silence. It is much more difficult to stand for Christ regardless of the opposition we face. Yet that is one of the few questions in life that truly matters.

During the Congress of the Cults, Richard Wurmbrand made that difficult decision to stand. When the opposition loomed ahead, this is what he discovered:

> The fear Richard felt during his abduction had departed. In its place was a hardened resolve to suffer anything for the sake of the gospel. Richard believed God would empower him to stand up to the worst physical agony his abductors could impart.
>
> Richard sat in silence. Motionless as the stones surrounding him, he began to thank God for bringing him to this prison. Each passing second became an answer to his and Sabina's prayers to let them bear a cross. What strange and wonderful opportunities would blossom within these walls? What friendships with the guards could he build? Richard didn't know. But he hoped God would shine through him as he suffered in isolation in the foreboding Calea Rahovei prison.[2]

It wasn't so different for Paul. Read what he wrote to his beloved fellow minister of the gospel, Timothy, in 2 Timothy 1:8–12.

There is no greater love or power known than that of Jesus's sacrifice that bought our deliverance from the prison of sin. Each of us has to decide whether we believe the message of redemption and whether it is worth living and dying for. What is it you believe?

What is it about carrying the cross that causes you to be afraid or ashamed?

What is it that causes you to pick up the cross even when you suffer opposition for taking that stand?

What are you utterly dependent on God to do so you can stand and bear the cross for his glory?

What is it about carrying the cross that fills you with hope and joy?

## Memorize

Therefore do not be ashamed of the testimony about our Lord, nor of me his prisoner, but share in suffering for the gospel by the power of God, who saved us and called us to a holy calling, not because of our works but because of his own purpose and grace, which he gave us in Christ Jesus before the ages began, and which now has been manifested through the appearing of our Savior Christ Jesus, who abolished death and

brought life and immortality to light through the
gospel, for which I was appointed a preacher and
apostle and teacher, which is why I suffer as I do.
But I am not ashamed, for I know whom I have
believed, and I am convinced that he is able to
guard until that day what has been entrusted to
me. (2 Tim. 1:8–12)

# I Will Take the Next Step

*I can develop an unshakable conviction to stand for Christ in the face
of any opposition.*

There is no question that there is a price—sometimes a dreadful
price—to be paid for following Jesus. It is, after all, a *cross* he asks
us to bear for him. At the same time, it isn't really hard to know
what God calls us to do. It isn't beyond the reach of any of us. In
fact, even a child can understand and respond in faith.

Count Zinzendorf, at the age of four, was taken
to an art gallery in Düsseldorf, Germany. He
stood before a picture of the crucified Christ. It
bore the inscription, "This I have done for you;
what are you doing for Me?"

Then and there, the little boy decided to
dedicate his life to the Savior.

He could never forget that question. While still a child he told himself, *A faith that does nothing is just babbling.*

When he was grown up, he formed the community of the Moravians, which has as its motto "The Savior deserves everything."[3]

Yes! Our Savior does deserve everything! When we truly believe this, we can be faithful to serve him with all we are and have. We can be confident that our sacrifices—however small and inadequate they may appear in the eyes of the world—will be enough. Consider the faithful testimony of two "uneducated, common men" in Acts 4:13–29.

What is it that makes an astonishing witness for Jesus?

How important is it to stand unashamed and firm in our testimony about Jesus?

How do we prepare ourselves to stand for Christ?

If you want to be an astonishing witness of Christ, then give yourself to God and let him use you!

# Standing Firm on the Word of God

The LORD is my light and my salvation;
>    whom shall I fear?
The LORD is the stronghold of my life;
>    of whom shall I be afraid?
When evildoers assail me
>    to eat up my flesh,
my adversaries and foes,
>    it is they who stumble and fall.
Though an army encamp against me,
>    my heart shall not fear;
though war arise against me,
>    yet I will be confident....
Teach me your way, O LORD,
>    and lead me on a level path
>    because of my enemies.
Give me not up to the will of my adversaries;
>    for false witnesses have risen against me,
>    and they breathe out violence.
I believe that I shall look upon the goodness of the LORD
>    in the land of the living!
Wait for the LORD;
>    be strong, and let your heart take courage;
>    wait for the LORD! (Ps. 27:1–3, 11–14)

# 2

# EVANGELIZING THE INVADERS

*When one Christian was sentenced to death, he was allowed to see his wife before being executed. His last words to his wife were, "You must know that I die loving those who kill me. They don't know what they do and my last request of you is to love them, too. Don't have bitterness in your heart because they killed your beloved one. We will meet in heaven." These words impressed the officer of the secret police who attended the discussion between the two. He later told me the story in prison where he had been sent for becoming a Christian.*

Richard Wurmbrand, *Tortured for Christ*

# Session Start-Up

## Let's Talk about That One

Talk about being a witness for Christ until your last breath! In what ways does this conversation differ from one you might have with your spouse, other family member, or close friend if you were in a similar circumstance?

Theirs is not a typical human response. What has to happen and what is the process that enables a person to grow into this kind of love—even for one's executioners?

What do you think it would mean to this Christian couple to know that their commitment to love the lost no matter what the cost not only had an impact on the official who was with them at the time but is still having an impact today?

## Let's Pray Together

*Dear Lord, it is hard for us even to imagine the depth of the cruelty and suffering our persecuted brothers and sisters have endured for remaining faithful to you. Their commitment to love and serve you with all they have—even seeking to love their tormentors as you do—is a powerful testimony to us and our walk of faith. Lord, we offer you both our tears and our praise for loving us enough to save us. We are blessed when you purify our hearts and cultivate your love in us so we love the lost as you do. Thank you for being our Savior, strength, and example. May our faithfulness in living for you and your purposes result in the salvation of the lost and bring honor to your name. In the name of Jesus we pray. Amen.*

# Video Exploration

## Video Notes

- Inspired by a passionate love for the lost
- The nightmare begins
- Greeting an invading army with the love of Christ
- Into the barracks to "buy a watch"
- Courage to change the subject
- Love enough to speak in the language of the lost
- A pastor's son prays for a second chance
- Love for the lost leads a Russian soldier to risk everything
- Our Spirit-empowered choice: forgive and love
- Respond with the love of Jesus in any circumstance

## Video Discussion

1. The "peaceful" takeover of Romania by a million Communist Russian troops in August 1944 initiated a nightmare of change, loss, and "reeducation" for the people. Some managed to flee or go into hiding. Those who remained—especially, but not exclusively, those who were known to be religious—were closely watched. For decades Christians, people who were not atheists, and even known atheists and party members were subject to surveillance, betrayal, arrest, beatings, and torture at any time for nearly any offense.

> What are our natural instincts when we are forced to live in that kind of hostile environment? (Note: Please do not answer these as rhetorical questions. The reality is closer to home than we might like to think. Many communities struggle to thrive through the chaos of natural disasters, political change, gang violence, cultural misunderstanding and conflict, and drug abuse.)

> What impact do you think the kind of instability experienced in Romania might have on how we live out our faith—how we love our neighbor, for example?

> If your community was to experience trauma and chaos, how do you think your relationships with people in your neighborhood, at school, or at work would change?

Do you think people would be more or less willing to hear the story of Jesus and his love? Explain.

Would you be more or less willing to reach out and share the love of Jesus with people, and why?

2. It is no secret that Richard greatly loved telling others about God and the salvation available through Jesus. He could speak Russian and, having spent time in Moscow, had developed a long-standing dream of sharing the love of Christ with the Russian people. How significant a factor do you think that dream was in determining his swift and bold actions following the Communist Russian takeover?

In what ways does Richard's prayerful thinking regarding future opportunities God might give him to reach out to the lost differ from how you approach what God might call you to accomplish in the future?

3. Every opportunity we have to share the message of Jesus comes with some risk. What do you think about the risk Richard took to go into the Russian barracks in order to share the gospel, and how willing are you to risk serious consequences in order to share the gospel?

Who are the risky people, what are the risky places for sharing the gospel in our communities, and what consequences might we face if we stand for Christ in those situations?

To what extent does God's love for people who do not know him burn in our hearts and compel us to step into risky situations to make his love known?

Thinking about the ways Richard used his understanding of Russian life to connect with his audience in the barracks, how can his example help you more effectively reach out to others with the good news of God's love and forgiveness?

4. In the face of persecution, the path of reaching out with the love of Christ is riddled with risk. Before the young Russian soldier ever stepped onto the train with a satchel of Bibles, he assessed that risk with the words, "If my life were my own, I would have quit already." How important is it for anyone who desires to love the lost as God does to live in light of that same perspective?

5. As a young Christian in Communist Czechoslovakia, Petr Jasek was afraid to speak about his Christian upbringing. But he allowed that lost opportunity to motivate him to build his faith and prayed for a future opportunity to stand boldly for Christ. How risky was that opportunity when it came, and how powerful was his response—not only for those who witnessed his stand, but for him and for us?

In light of his commitment to prepare to stand for Christ, what do you realize about your own readiness to reach out to others and share the story of Jesus?

# Growing into a More Biblical Faith Perspective

## Our Study Together

When the Russian army rolled into Romania, Richard and Sabina knew there would be trouble ahead. The beatings they had already endured under the Nazis were severe but paled in comparison to the cruelties the Communists would inflict. The Communists introduced the greatest carnage the world had ever witnessed, claiming nearly one hundred million lives.

Yet the Lord had prepared Richard and Sabina for the horror ahead. Living in Nazi-controlled Romania prepared them to carry out their Christian work in secret. They learned that with the help of the Holy Spirit they could withstand any amount of torture and forgive their enemies. No matter how excruciating, humiliating, or degrading the physical and psychological abuse Communism inflicted on them, it could be endured, and they could love those who inflicted it. Christ had been tortured for them, and he would assist them when they were tortured for him.[1]

We can look at the experiences of Richard and Sabina and thousands of other persecuted and tortured Romanian believers and weep for their suffering, marvel at their willingness to endure, and be inspired by their faithfulness to tell others the good news about Jesus. But we fall short in our understanding of what God wants to accomplish in and through us if we do not also consider their love. Their love for their Savior. Their love for the lost. And yes, even their love for those who hated them and relentlessly inflicted the most brutal and degrading torments on them.

Consider, for example, Richard's story of love transformed:

> Richard knew he was becoming a broken man. During his time imprisoned in Calea Rahovei, the guards broke four of his vertebrae and many other bones. His skin was carved up, split apart, and scarred over from repeated knife attacks. Eighteen holes were burned into his muscle tissue. His malnourished frame and lack of sleep

compromised his immunity. Pneumonia became
a constant threat. Every day at dusk, Richard lay
half dead in his cell, mustering up what little
strength he could to prepare for the torture that
came at dawn.

Yet even in his brokenness, he discovered a
healing he had never before felt. With each interaction with the guards, he felt anger and hatred
leave his body. Somehow suffering was producing
sympathy. Unlike many of the other prisoners
who spoke spitefully about the interrogators,
Richard began to love them. He determined that
God would judge him based not on how much
torture he could take but instead on how well he
could love his torturers.[2]

The supernatural love of God abiding in a human heart is the
most powerful weapon of goodness and transformation there is.
Let's delve into what the Bible says about God's love so that we too
may diligently cultivate it in our hearts and reach out to the lost as
bold witnesses of his love and forgiveness.

1. True love, the kind of love that will sacrifice itself for the benefit
of another, begins with God who is love. In what ways does God's
love differ from all other loves (Rom. 5:6–8; 1 John 4:7–10)?

What crucial transformation of life perspective and motivation does the love of Jesus make in the hearts and lives of those who follow him (2 Cor. 5:14–15)?

2. What example does Jesus provide of what it means to live for him rather than ourselves, especially when we face the sting of insults, persecution, and injustice (1 Pet. 2:21–24)?

As much as we may desire and strive to successfully follow in the steps of Jesus, we will fall short, but what one thing can we rely on to enable us to live for him (1 John 4:15–17)?

3. When Jesus summarized the Ten Commandments, which God gave to show Israel how to live as his chosen people and make his love known to others, what did he list as being most important (Matt. 22:37–40)?

What do you think Jesus wanted people to realize about the power and testimony of love when he said that all other commandments depend on these two?

What happens when we try to do what God desires in the world but lack love for him and others?

4. His unsurpassed love made Jesus willing to be the sin sacrifice for all humanity. But Jesus clearly recognized how radical and counterintuitive the nature of God's love is to those who follow him—especially when we encounter those who do us harm. Because Jesus wanted his disciples to learn to live and love as he did, he taught them what the love of God looks like as it is lived out in a sinful world. Carefully read his teaching in Matthew 5:43–48 and Luke 6:27–36, and list the key responses of God's love in action (in both passages) that Jesus says are appropriate when people hate, oppose, and mistreat us.

Why are these responses necessary if we intend to be living examples of the character and love of God within us (Matt. 5:48; Luke 6:35–36)?

5. If we are limited to understanding life only as the world sees it, Jesus has given his followers a difficult road to walk. But Jesus did not leave his followers ill-prepared for the journey. What message of warning did Jesus give to everyone who is faithful to love him above all else (John 15:18–21)?

In what ways do these words of Jesus explain the violence inflicted on Christians in Romanian prisons, and in what ways are they also an encouragement to not only endure but to triumph in love?

I have seen Christians in Communist prisons with fifty pounds of chains on their feet, tortured with red-hot iron pokers, in whose throats spoonfuls of salt had been forced, being kept afterward without water, starving, whipped, suffering from cold—and praying with fervor for the Communists. This is humanly inexplicable! It is the love of Christ which was poured out in our hearts.… It was in prison that we found the hope of salvation for the Communists.

It was there that we developed a sense of
responsibility toward them. It was in being tortured by them that we learned to love them.[3]

To what degree do these supernatural sacrifices of love communicate the reality, power, and love of God in the world and
for the lost?

6. Of his fellow prisoners, Richard wrote, "A flower, if you bruise
it under your feet, rewards you by giving you its perfume. Likewise
Christians, tortured by the Communists, rewarded their torturers
by love. We brought many of our jailors to Christ. And we are
dominated by one desire: to give Communists who have made us
suffer the best we have, the salvation that comes from our Lord
Jesus Christ."[4]

Now read Ephesians 5:1–2 together and talk about what such a
sacrifice motivated by love—for God and for the lost—means
to God.

In what ways does the prisoners' example of life lived in
love expand your practical understanding of 1 Corinthians
16:13–14?

## Make It Personal

We may be inclined to think that the time persecuted Christians spend in prison is not well spent, that it is lost to the benefit of God's kingdom. Perhaps this assumption is a lie the Enemy desperately hopes we will believe. It certainly is not the truth. In fact, for the Wurmbrands and many of their fellow believers, the prisons of Romania may have been one of the best places to boldly and creatively evangelize the invaders.

In prison, the darkness of anger, fear, hatred, and vengeance often rules the hearts of prisoners and guards alike. In contrast, the sincere love of God that prompts great and seemingly unrewarded sacrifice for the benefit of others cannot be dimmed. The love of God in the heart of believers who reach out to share the good news of Jesus cannot be silenced.

Richard Wurmbrand wrote of a young girl who, in wisdom far beyond her years, said, "If someone wanted to kill me … I would say to him, 'First, let me tell you the story of Jesus.' If he killed me afterward, at least I'd go to heaven."[5] This is the priority of God's love brought to life in the actions of persecuted Christians around the world who face torturers and executioners: first, let me tell you about Jesus; then, I will continue to live out God's love no matter what comes.

None of us has ultimate control over our life circumstances. For many, there is little chance that we will be abducted and hidden away, tormented in prison for years. But we don't know the character of our new neighbor, coworker, or classmate. We don't know if he or she will welcome or oppose God's gift of salvation through Jesus. We do, however, know God's way of living and reaching out to the lost. Read Romans 12:9–12, 14, 17–21 in light of how you live out God's love in your world.

How sincere is your love for God and others, and in what ways may it be lacking?

To what extent are your thoughts and actions focused on honoring, blessing, and living at peace with others so you may win an opportunity to share with them the love of God made available through Jesus?

What change of heart will you pray for in order to "step up" your testimony of love to those who are threatening or difficult to love?

## Memorize

For the love of Christ controls us, because we have concluded this: that one has died for all, therefore all have died; and he died for all, that those who live might no longer live for themselves but for him who for their sake died and was raised. (2 Cor. 5:14–15)

# I Will Take the Next Step

*I can reach out boldly and creatively. I can be a witness for Christ no matter the cost.*

Not one of us knows when God will give us an unexpected opportunity to make his love and salvation known to one of his lost children who desperately needs him. It may be, as it was for Petr Jasek, a teacher who asks what your father's occupation is. It may be a face-to-face encounter with someone who hates Christians and everything they stand for. It may be a new immigrant neighbor or a fellow soldier.

The question for us is, how strong is the love of Christ in our hearts? Is it powerful enough to compel us to act despite our fears or objections? Will we fulfill God's desire that we love each person as he does? How much of a risk will we take to demonstrate God's love and make his offer of salvation known?

And what will we do if responding to a God-given opportunity might cost us everything? A long time ago, God presented such an opportunity to a follower of Jesus named Ananias. Acts 9:1–2, 10–22 tells the rest of the story.

Ananias knew the risk. Saul was going to Damascus with authority to arrest any Christians he found. Obedience to God could cost Ananias his life. Why do you think he followed through?

Would you have had the love to do the same? Why?

The transformation in Saul (later, Paul) was astonishing! People could scarcely believe it. What message did he immediately begin sharing, and what impact did it have?

In what ways may God be calling you to love him and others in a big, and perhaps costly, way?

How ready and willing are you to step out and "love big"?

# Standing Firm on the Word of God

> For while we were still weak, at the right time
> Christ died for the ungodly. For one will
> scarcely die for a righteous person—though
> perhaps for a good person one would dare even
> to die—but God shows his love for us in that
> while we were still sinners, Christ died for us.
> (Rom. 5:6–8)

Even though I walk through the valley of the shadow of death,
    I will fear no evil,
for you are with me;
    your rod and your staff,
    they comfort me.
You prepare a table before me
    in the presence of my enemies;
you anoint my head with oil;
    my cup overflows.
Surely goodness and mercy shall follow me
    all the days of my life,
and I shall dwell in the house of the LORD
    forever. (Ps. 23:4–6)

# 3

# THE UNDERGROUND CHURCH

*Finally, near the end of the visit, Sabina's name was called. When she saw her son, she forgot she was a prisoner, forgot what she looked like, forgot where she was, and simply embraced him with her eyes. How thin he was, and how serious! She gazed at him, and he at her, and in a flash the fifteen minutes had passed. They barely spoke, but near the end of the visit and across the thirty feet separating mother from son, Sabina called, "Mihai, believe in Jesus with all your heart!"*

The Voice of the Martyrs, *Wurmbrand*

# Session Start-Up

## Let's Talk about That One

What do a mother and son say when they haven't seen or communicated with one another for years, when they both know they may never see each other again, when they remain separated by ten yards, and hostile guards evaluate their every word?

Imagine how hard that would be! What would you want to say to your child or hear from your parent?

Sabina had no way of knowing if her teenage son, who had lost both of his parents to imprisonment because of their Christian faith, still held onto his faith or if the Communists had stolen the loyalty of his heart and mind. In response to her plea for faith, he shouted back, "Mother, if you can still believe in a place like this … then so must I."[1] What does Sabina and Mihai's interaction reveal about the significance of even one sentence of God's truth spoken in love to encourage a fellow believer?

How faithful are we to make the most of the fellowship we share with other believers—in our faith community and around the world—by encouraging, teaching, praying, and standing with our family in Christ?

## Let's Pray Together

*Dear Lord Jesus, we have grown so accustomed to being self-sufficient and self-absorbed that it is hard to think of ourselves and our fellow believers as being a community—an interdependent family of brothers and sisters united by faith to love and serve you and one another. Lord, help us to know you, learn your ways, and discover the fullness of life lived in fellowship with you and the great family of people who follow you. Give us your heart of love, not only for the lost but for our believing family. May we be faithful to share the gifts of your Spirit in blessing one another. The gift of love to cover our sins against one another with forgiveness. Joy to share with those who rejoice. Peace for those troubled by worry or fear. Patience for those who irritate us. Kindness for those who are looked down upon. Goodness for those who are in need. Gentleness for those who are wounded. Faithfulness for those who struggle. Self-control to remember that we live to serve you and not ourselves. In the blessed name of Jesus our Savior we ask this. Amen.*

# Video Exploration

## Video Notes

- Our testimony of love for one another
- The church under assault
- Surviving and serving through the under-ground church
- God bless you!
- Taking the risk to gather together
- Paying the price to continue the work of Christ
- Willing to invest ourselves for the benefit of others?
- What are we missing?
- Better together!

## Video Discussion

1. In parts of the world, Christians have the opportunity to gather together for prayer, worship, fellowship, and teaching without restraint, interference, or reprisal. In other places, such as the Wurmbrands experienced in Romania, those who meet together risk imprisonment and torture. What was so important about meeting and ministering together that the Wurmbrands and their fellow believers were willing to take the risks they did to gather in fellowship together?

2. What do you value most about the congregation of believers with whom you gather for fellowship, prayer, Bible study, out-reach, and worship?

Is sharing your life of faith with other believers valuable enough to risk dying for? Why or why not?

To what extent do you count on one another for encourage-ment, strength in the Word of God, help in the hardships you face, support in demonstrating Christ's love in a hostile world, and companionship that reminds you of how much God loves you? What pleases or concerns you about your answer?

3. Consider the children who approached the Russian soldiers and begged for gum, then gave them a blessing. In even that one, small act, how important do you think the house church community was in making their action possible?

For example, do you think the children would have done it if they had been one instead of three? Why or why not?

How important do you think the encouragement, teaching, and example of the adult believers was to the children's continued activity to reach out in love to their enemies?

4. When we think about being a witness to the world around us, we tend to think of more effective evangelism methods, how to bridge cultural divides, and perhaps the message our lifestyle communicates to the lost. These are important, but there is an aspect that is often overlooked and underappreciated.

How often do we consider the message our attitudes and behaviors toward our fellow believers send out into the world?

What, for example, does our stubborn infighting and vehement criticism or even condemnation of other believers communicate about our loving, forgiving God and the people who claim to belong to his holy, sanctified family?

How well does our gossip—"Do you know what I heard about ...?"—or even our casual, negative comments—"Of course, what would you expect from ...?"—represent a body of Christ that is to welcome sinners with the sincere love of God?

What does our judgement or lack of patient, prayerful, faithful care and support for the ongoing needs of families who struggle—perhaps with debilitating physical or mental illness, addiction, death, or financial challenges—say about how well we love one another? About how accurately we represent the loving and compassionate heart of God and his desire to bless his creation?

5. What message do we, as participants in Christ's body in the world, really want to convey to one another and send to people who do not know the hope and love that can be found in God's forgiveness?

What changes in heart and behavior toward one another would bring us closer to fulfilling God's purposes for his church?

# Growing into a More Biblical Faith Perspective

## Our Study Together

When Sabina was released from prison, her son Mihai greeted her with words she would never forget: "Mother, I'm on your side, and I love the Lord."

His greeting was possible in large part because of years of faithful service and sacrifice by "Aunt Alice" who unofficially adopted eleven-year-old Mihai when Sabina was imprisoned. No stranger to punishment for one's loyalty to Christ, Alice had been relieved of her position as head of an important teaching department because she refused to join the Communist Party. She managed to eke out a living by teaching French and helping students prepare for their examinations. But it took every penny she earned to provide for herself, her aging father, and Mihai in the one room they called home. Alice also intervened and cared for other disenfranchised children whose parents had been killed or imprisoned, saving them from life on the streets, hunger, or death from exposure.

When other believers learned of her service and needs, they too sacrificed. The underground church never forgot its duty to protect children who had been orphaned. One elderly couple managed to travel undetected for two days to give Alice a large sum of money. Mrs. Mihailovici traveled hundreds of miles to give Alice one bag of potatoes. It was all she had, and she gave everything. When the militia learned what she had done, they beat her so badly she never recovered from her injuries.[2]

No matter how great the sacrifice, whether it was worshipping in secret with a small gathering of believers, suffering daily nearly to the point of death in prison, taking the risk of welcoming unknown new believers into their fellowship, or covertly printing and distributing portions of the Bible, many who followed Jesus remained faithful to their commitment to Christ and to one another. Through their faith community that became known as the underground church, believers continued to follow the biblical mandate to fellowship together, meet one another's needs, and support one another in advancing God's kingdom under the threat of fierce persecution.

Why were they willing to sacrifice so much? Let's take a closer look at what the Bible teaches about the life and work God has ordained for the community of people who follow him and see what we discover. Our Christian family may be far more important and necessary to our walk of faith than we realize.

1. As humans born into sin, we crave independence and the right to decide what works for us. We desire what relationships can provide yet demand freedom from the constraints of those relationships. This is not the harmony God intends for his creation, especially for his family—those who are redeemed from bondage to sin by the shed blood of Jesus. Relationships in the family of God aren't built on our ideas of what life should be. A life lived for Christ must be built on faithful obedience to his teaching and example.

What foundational principle did Jesus establish for relationships between those who would follow him (John 13:12–17, 34–35)?

How did Paul describe the relationship of individual members of the community of Jesus followers to the Corinthians (1 Cor. 12:12–13, 21–27)?

When it comes to our behavior in relationship to others in the body of Christ, what guiding principle expresses our obedience to Christ and our love and concern for one another (1 Cor. 10:24)?

2. Acts 2:42–47 describes the life of fellowship that followers of Jesus enjoyed after Pentecost. What were their priorities, what characterized their relationships, and how did their ministry impact others around them?

3. Paul's letters to the churches he planted provide a wealth of teaching and examples of how the family of God is to live together in love. Read Colossians 3:12–17; 4:2–6 and list the attitudes, virtues, and actions that Paul said are to characterize the fellowship of believers.

What difference do you think the intentional development of these qualities and actions would have on the life and fellowship of your family, group, and/or church?

4. No matter how good and humble our intent, we must remember that no fellowship of believers is perfect. We will have to deal with conflict, sin, failure, and disappointment within the body of Christ. But these difficulties do not change who we live for or how we are to love, encourage, and support our family in Christ. The early church had to deal with conflict too, and at one point the apostles and elders gathered together to resolve an intensely divisive issue related to the law of Moses and Gentile believers.

Read Acts 15:22–35, which records their resolution. Notice how the apostles and elders approached the issue in their response, how it was received, and how they continued—as the body of Christ—to build up one another in love and service to their Lord.

What do you think is important for us to learn from their example?

5. The early church was an impassioned, faithful community of believers who were devoted to obedience to God and supported one another in their faith commitment. What do we learn about their faithfulness as a community to make the gospel known and how they supported and encouraged one another in that endeavor (Acts 4:5–7, 13, 18–33)?

What specific things can we do to better encourage one another in the work of God's kingdom?

6. One day when Sabina was out walking, a little man with thinning hair stared at her intently as they approached one another and then passed. When she next put her hand into her coat pocket, she found a folded note he had slipped in unnoticed. It read, "It shall come to pass in the day the LORD gives you rest from your sorrow, and from your fear and the hard bondage in which you were made to serve."

"I knew that the fight continued," she wrote. "Perhaps it was not on show, but everywhere around me was the love of God. In passing faces that betrayed nothing. In hearts that no Stalin could touch. A new happiness flowed through me. I was a member of the Underground Church."[3]

> It often takes just a little effort to encourage a brother or sister in Christ who carries a heavy burden. What are some of the simple, practical, everyday ways by which you can reach out to another believer and fulfill the admonition of 1 Thessalonians 5:11?

7. Prayer is one of the most powerful weapons followers of Jesus have to accomplish God's work on earth. And prayer for one another is one of the greatest gifts we can share with our family in Christ, particularly for our brothers and sisters who face persecution and imprisonment. What kinds of things did believers in the early church pray for one another (Rom. 15:30–32; Phil. 1:9–14, 19–21)?

> What ideas do we gain from their example that can help us more effectively pray for our family in Christ?

What impact did the power of prayer demonstrated in Acts 12:1–7, 11–17 have on Peter and the believers who were praying for him?

In what ways does their experience of earnest prayer for a fellow believer cause you to think differently about your prayers for your fellow believers?

## Make It Personal

One day, when Richard was visiting a Christian brother in a provincial town, six men from the West came to visit him. The men participated with a Christian organization that provided secret relief work for families of Christian martyrs and also smuggled in Christian literature. Filled with joy, Richard wrote:

> My joy was in knowing that they had come and that we were no longer forgotten. Steady, regular help began to come to the Underground Church. By secret channels we got many Bibles and other Christian literature, as well as relief for families of Christian martyrs. Now, with their help, we of the Underground Church could work much better.

It was not only that they gave us the Word of God, but we saw that we were beloved. They brought us a word of comfort. During the years of brainwashing, we had heard, "Nobody loves you anymore, nobody loves you anymore, nobody loves you anymore." Now we saw American and English Christians who risked their lives to show us that they loved us....

The value of the Bibles smuggled in by these means cannot be understood by an American or an English Christian who "swims" in Bibles.

My family and I would not have survived without the material help I received from praying Christians abroad.... For us, these believers were like angels sent by God![4]

When we have freedom to worship and share our faith, when we have access to God's Word whenever we want it, and when our basic physical needs are satisfied, we may not remember our brothers and sisters who suffer and endure for the gospel of Christ. But 1 Corinthians 12:26 reminds us that we cannot separate ourselves from our family in faith, no matter how distant they may be: "If one member suffers, all suffer together; if one member is honored, all rejoice together."

Read Hebrews 13:1, 3; then read 2 Corinthians 1:8–11; 7:5–7.

In what ways do these accounts—from the Bible and the life of Richard Wurmbrand—give you a better understanding of how important your family in Christ is to you and you to them?

How much do these accounts motivate you to step up your actions to remember, love, pray for, and in other ways serve your persecuted family in Christ?

What are you willing to do differently in your daily life in order to bless your family in Christ—those in your immediate faith fellowship as well as those who live far away—through prayer, support, and encouragement?

## Memorize

> So if there is any encouragement in Christ, any comfort from love, any participation in the Spirit, any affection and sympathy, complete my joy by being of the same mind, having the same love, being in full accord and of one mind. Do nothing from selfish ambition or conceit, but in humility count others more significant than yourselves. Let each of you look not only to his own interests, but also to the interests of others. (Phil. 2:1–4)

# I Will Take the Next Step

*I can advance God's eternal kingdom through obedience to God's instruction to encourage and serve other believers.*

In his later years, Richard wrote fondly of his grandchildren and their growing understanding of life and faith. In one account he wrote, "Amelie remained in the house as we accompanied departing guests to the car. Within minutes she joined us, saying, 'I was afraid that if I remained alone I might do something stupid.'" Richard continued with this observation: "People are especially prone to doing stupid things when they are on their own and unobserved. But why should they be alone? There are no loners in God's service. Christians should remain in constant fellowship with their brethren."[5]

The Bible provides abundant evidence of God stepping in when his people were alone. Think of how often God told those who serve him, "I am with you." Think of the many times the Bible tells us that God sent a messenger, a prophet, a companion—an angel—because his people were vulnerable to deception, discouragement, or disobedience. God loves his creation and from the very beginning has known "it is not good that the man should be alone" (Gen. 2:18).

After Jesus was crucified, his disciples struggled on their own, feeling confusion and doubt, until Jesus came to them in his resurrected body and continued his ministry with them. And when Jesus did leave this earth to take his place on heaven's throne, he promised to send the Comforter, the Holy Spirit, to be with them and guide them. Thank God for his guiding hand! The gentle corrections of our Good Shepherd keep us from the innumerable perils that the Enemy, our sinful nature, and the fallen world continually lead us toward.

We see the pattern of fellowship, community, encouragement, mutual support, and sacrificial service to one another continuing in the early Christian church. Paul, for example, traveled from city to city sharing the gospel with Jews and Gentiles in the Roman world. The fledgling communities of new believers he left behind were both a constant blessing and a source of concern for him. Despite the distances and communication limitations of the time, Paul kept in constant contact with these communities, encouraging them to remain faithful when they faced persecution and sending them teachers and support from other communities of believers.

Paul spent a very short time teaching in Thessalonica before riotous unrest forced him to flee into the night. But he did not forget about the Thessalonian believers. His letters to them provide an intimate picture of his deep love, spiritual nurturing, and practical care for his Christian family. In fact, part of his letter reads, "For this reason, when I could bear it no longer, I sent to learn about your faith, for fear that somehow the tempter had tempted you" (1 Thess. 3:5).

It seems Paul was deeply concerned about the spiritual welfare of the Thessalonian believers. He recognized their vulnerability and feared that left alone they might stumble in their walk with God. So he worked to strengthen their faith and ensure that what he had done to advance God's kingdom in that community would continue.

Now read 1 Thessalonians 3:1–13, one of Paul's letters to his Christian family in Thessalonica. Take note of his great love and support for his brothers and sisters in faith. Consider also your need to receive and your desire to demonstrate love and concern for the community of Jesus followers where you live and around the world.

What "stupid things" am I at risk for doing in my walk of faith when I am alone and not in regular fellowship with a community of Jesus followers?

To what extent does God want me to rely on my fellow believers to be with me, to teach me, and to hold me accountable to faithfully follow Jesus?

How important is it for me to share in the lives of other Jesus followers? To share in their hope? To pray with them? To prepare for and support one another during times of hardship and persecution? To work for and rejoice in the advancement of God's kingdom?

What specific things can I do to stand with my fellow believers during their struggles?

For which of my fellow believers' needs will I actively pray?

What can I share or do that will bless my fellow believers?

In what specific ways am I allowing my brothers and sisters in Christ to strengthen and encourage my walk of faith?

# Standing Firm on the Word of God

And let us consider how to stir up one another to love and good works, not neglecting to meet together, as is the habit of some, but encouraging one another, and all the more as you see the Day drawing near. (Heb. 10:24–25)

# 4

# LEAP YEAR

*I received the grace from the Lord and strength to act according to Christ's words. When someone hits you on one cheek, to turn him the other one. I think it's a supernatural love and a supernatural peace that I could have despite these physical attacks. I was sincerely praying for them that the Lord Jesus would reveal himself as the Lord and Savior and God for them. That was my sincere prayer. The more that I was praying for them the easier, actually, it was.*

Petr Jasek, Global Ambassador, The Voice of the Martyrs

# Session Start-Up

## Let's Talk about That One

Petr, a Christian from the Czech Republic, had been sentenced to life in prison in Sudan. Held in a crowded cell with a half dozen hardened ISIS fighters and sympathizers, he received brutal beatings—and worse—from his cellmates. What would be foremost in your thoughts and feelings if you faced what he did?


We can be sure that some of the same thoughts and feelings we might experience were on Petr's mind as well. But that wasn't all. He remembered God's Word and chose to respond with love rather than anger or retaliation. Like Richard and Sabina Wurmbrand, he fervently prayed for those who tormented him. In such circumstances, when grave peril looms over every breath we take, what do you think is the secret to remembering and obeying God's Word?


## Let's Pray Together

*Dear Lord, you are our loving Creator who has washed away our sin with the blood of Jesus so that we can stand before you as if our sin never happened. Thank you, Lord. We love you and want to stand faithfully for you at all times—even in a crisis. But we cannot do this by our own strength and will. We come to you needing you to transform our hearts, so they will become more like yours. We invite you to purify and fill our hearts until they overflow with the truth and grace of your Word. Empower us by the love and power of your Spirit to overcome every impulse to respond to our suffering according to our own feelings and in our own strength. Make the desires of your heart ours. Teach us to remember and obey your Word so we may love the lost as you love them. In the name of Jesus we pray. Amen.*

# Video Exploration

## Video Notes

- Prepare for the privilege of suffering for Christ
- Know what God has said
- A verse for this very day!
- Responding to terrifying fear in the strength of God's Word
- Petr Jasek—his homecoming delayed
- We want you to live … and suffer
- Living out God's Word is not about knowing the right answer
- God gives supernatural love and peace to pray for those who harm us
- What is your foundation for living out your faith?

## Video Discussion

1. All of us know what it means to prepare for what we expect will happen in the future. We prepare for tests in school. We prepare to celebrate holidays and major life events like birthdays and weddings. We prepare for storms and natural disasters. We prepare for retirement. What did you think when you learned that Richard and Sabina prepared for what they considered to be inevitable—bearing the cross of persecution, imprisonment, and torture because of their faith?

What are your first thoughts as to how you would prepare yourself, and your loved ones, for future persecution?

Do you agree that preparations of the type Richard and Sabina made really matter? Why or why not?

If you asked them, to what extent would other believers in your family, group, or church join you in preparing to face opposition and even suffering for the cause of Christ? Discuss what you think would be an appropriate way to respond to their answers.

2. The prison experiences of Richard Wurmbrand and, more recently, Petr Jasek are a powerful testimony to the power of God's Word at work in the hearts and actions of faithful believers.

In what ways have their experiences as presented in the video changed your perspective on the power of God's Word?

How important do you think it is for every follower of Jesus to know and live out the teachings of God's Word every day—not just when in prison or facing other extreme situations?

3. When we face difficult circumstances of any degree, we choose how we respond. We can choose to operate out of our fallen human nature or according to what God has said.

If you are willing, share about a time when you relied on God's Word to guide your response to a difficult circumstance. In what way(s) did choosing that response enable you to live out your faith and overcome your trial in a way that brought honor to God?

Share about a time when you responded to a difficult situation according to your human nature. As you consider the ways that choice affected how you live out your faith and represent God's kingdom to others, would you say you "got it right" or did you "get it wrong"?

What are your thoughts about the impact our biblical choices versus human nature choices have on people who don't know, follow, or even believe there is a God?

4. In what specific ways do Richard and Petr's choices to rely on God's Word during their prison experiences encourage you in your faith walk?

What did they demonstrate that challenges you to grow not only in your knowledge of God's Word but how you apply it and allow it to mold your heart and mind?

# Growing into a More Biblical Faith Perspective

## Our Study Together

Try to imagine how shocking it would be to walk down the street and in an instant become utterly and completely powerless, abducted or arrested by people who do not have your best interests in mind. Suddenly you don't control whether you stand or sit, walk or run, take a step or fall on your face. Others decide if you will see your surroundings or be blindfolded. They decide if, when, and what you will eat and when and if you will sleep. You go from living a normal life to not being able to sip water or scratch your head if they do not permit it, and you have no idea if you will ever experience your definition of "normal" life again.

How disorienting and frightening would an experience like that be? How is it possible to think straight in such circumstances? Yet that is what Richard and Petr, and millions of other followers of Jesus have faced.

No wonder Richard and Sabina Wurmbrand planned and worked hard to prepare themselves to stand for Christ in the extremely difficult circumstances they expected to face. They decided that being faithful to Jesus was paramount—no matter what the cost—and they knew they had to be ready for whatever that commitment might require of them. They had confidence the eternal Word of God would give them hope to cling to and a solid foundation on which to stand and endure whatever might happen, so they learned as much of it as they could.

Like the apostle Paul who, undaunted, said to his fellow believers that he was "ready not only to be imprisoned but even to die … for the name of the Lord Jesus" (Acts 21:13), Richard and Sabina were ready. They armed themselves with the Word of God, and it served them and the cause of Christ well. Let's consider what the Bible reveals about the power of God's Word to sustain and guide us during times of crisis.

1. If we are not personally facing the pressure of intense persecution, we might assume that our spiritual knowledge, experience, and wisdom are sufficient to live faithfully for Christ. But that is in no way true. When it comes to living out our faith as disciples of Jesus—whether our circumstances are peaceful or tumultuous and threatening—we are fighting a spiritual battle. There is nothing casual or insignificant about it. We are fighting a real and powerful Enemy in order to advance God's kingdom, and it requires everything we have, but we do not fight alone. Where does our example, power, and help come from (Heb. 12:1–3)?

On what foundation did Jesus stand to fight the spiritual battles he faced on earth (Matt. 4:1–11)?

If Jesus relied on what God has said (what is written) in his battles against the Evil One, how well do you think we will do if we try to live out our faith on the basis of our own wisdom and the power of our own words?

2. As was true for Jesus, the Word of God is the foundation for how we express our faith through our thoughts, priorities, and actions in everyday life. When we read or hear the Word of God, what are we supposed to do with it, and what difference does it make in our walk of faith (James 1:22–25; 1 John 2:3–6)?

Knowing the Word of God is about understanding and experiencing it in a way that gets into our hearts and shapes the way we live out our faith. By what process does the Word of God become effective in the lives of those who desire to live a godly life, and why is this so important (Col. 3:15–17; 2 Tim. 3:12–17)?

3. During her days of forced labor, when even Communists were being imprisoned by their comrades, Sabina noted:

Those of us who had faith realized for the first time how rich we were. The youngest Christians and the weakest had more resources to call on than the wealthiest old ladies and the most brilliant intellectuals.

People with good brains, education, wit, when deprived of their books and concerts, often seemed to dry up like indoor plants exposed to the winds. Heart and mind were empty....

After work, women came to religious prisoners and asked, begged, even, to be told something of what we remembered from the Bible. The words gave hope, comfort, life.

We had no Bible. We ourselves hungered for it more than bread. How I wished I'd learned more of it by heart! But the passages we knew we repeated daily and at night, when we held vigils for prayer. Other Christians, like me, had deliberately committed long passages to memory, knowing that soon their turn would come for arrest. They brought riches to prison. While others quarreled and fought, we lay on our mattresses and used the Bible for prayer and meditation, and repeated its verses to ourselves through the long nights. We learned what newcomers brought and taught them what we knew. In this way an unwritten Bible circulated through all of Romania's prisons.[1]

In what way were Sabina and the other Christian prisoners obeying the teaching of Romans 15:1–4?

Would you have expected God's Word to be so important, providing comfort and hope even to prisoners who did not know him? Explain.

Read the following passages from Psalm 119, in which the psalmist overflowed in praise for the rich ministry and blessings of God's Word. Discuss how Sabina's experience of sharing God's Word in prison reflects the psalmist's experience of the Word (Ps. 119:140–144, 172–175).

4. Richard understood the power words could hold over the mind. He had spent years memorizing and repeating Scripture verses. After years of listening to repetitive Communist slogans, "Communism is good. Christianity is stupid. Give up! Give up!" for seventeen hours a day, he discovered a weapon more formidable than even brainwashing—*heart*washing." He goes on to explain, "The head always obeys the heart, and if Jesus Christ has cleansed the heart, the brain is sure to follow. 'For out of the abundance of the heart his mouth speaks' (Luke 6:45)."[2]

Perhaps the concept of heartwashing is best understood in the context of 2 Peter 1:1–8. Read this passage with the understanding that the "knowledge" of God and his "promises" represent what God says. How would you express what heartwashing is in your own words?

What encouragement do you think this passage offers to Christians in active ministry who suddenly are imprisoned, such as Richard and Petr were?

How did both men add these qualities to their faith and remain effective and productive in their knowledge (experience) of Christ during their time in prison?

In what ways would the following passages of God's Word cleanse the heart from the effects of brainwashing and promote heartwashing (Ps. 25:4–5; 119:30–32, 65–70, 92–95)?

## Make It Personal

Those of us who are privileged to have unrestricted access to God's Word cannot imagine how precious it is to our persecuted brothers and sisters in Christ. When they are imprisoned for their faith, access to the Bible is an unheard-of blessing. Perhaps a glimpse into life in room 4 of Tirgul-Ocna, Romania's prison sanatorium, will help us better understand what our persecuted family experiences.

After years of torture and abuse, Richard became so weak and ill with tuberculosis that he was transferred to Tirgul-Ocna and placed in room 4, the "death room." No one who went into that room came out alive. It was reserved for prisoners whose death was considered imminent. Richard, however, lived in that room for thirty months.

During Richard's time in room 4, scores of men were brought in and died, but not one died an atheist! It was amazing to witness Fascists, Communists, priests, unbelievers, saints, murderers, thieves, rich, and poor all making peace with God and man before they took their last breath. Amazing also was the gift Avram Radonovici brought into the room. He had been a music critic and could hum long scores of music which was greatly appreciated. But he had an even greater gift to share. Because of the way tuberculosis had affected his spine, a plaster cast encased his chest and torso. Richard wrote of this:

> As we watched he pushed a hand into the breast of this grey shell and extracted a small, tattered book. None of us had seen a book of any kind for years. Avram lay there quietly turning the pages, until he became conscious of the eager eyes fixed on him.
>
> "Your book," I said. "What is it? Where did you get it?"

"It's the Gospel according to John," said Avram. "I managed to hide it in my cast when the police came for me." He smiled. "Would you like to borrow it?"

I took the little book in my hands as if it were a live bird. No life-saving drug could have been more precious to me. I, who had known much of the Bible by heart and had taught it in the seminary, was forgetting it every day....

The Gospel went from hand to hand. It was difficult to give it up....

Many learned the Gospel by heart and we discussed it every day among ourselves; but we had to be careful which prisoners were let into the secret.[3]

In what ways does this part of Richard's story help you to understand the value of God's Word, especially when followers of Jesus face persecution?

How deeply does God's Word touch your heart, and how intensely do you long to read, study, and know it more fully?

In what way does Psalm 19:7–11 help you to see a more complete picture of the life-giving value of God's Word?

To what extent has this study expanded your understanding of and appreciation for God's Word and its role in living out your faith?

Are you willing to be seriously intentional about preparing for life's difficulties, including opposition and persecution, by studying and memorizing Scripture? Willing enough to start doing it today?

## Memorize

Jesus answered him, "If anyone loves me, he will keep my word, and my Father will love him, and we will come to him and make our home with him.... These things I have spoken to you while I am still with you. But the Helper, the Holy Spirit, whom the Father will send in my name, he will teach you all things and bring to your remembrance all that I have said to you. Peace I leave with you; my peace I give to you. Not as the world gives do I give to you.

Let not your hearts be troubled, neither let them be afraid." (John 14:23, 25–27)

# I Will Take the Next Step

*I can overcome trials through knowing and applying the living Word of God.*

With a permanent population of 200,000 men and women of all ages suffering for their faith in Romanian prisons and labor camps, Richard knew that he would, at some point, be called to join them. So he spent years preparing himself for that time. He had discovered 366 verses dealing with fear—one for every day of the year, including February 29 for leap year.

It is amazing to realize that Richard was abducted on February 29. He diligently prepared to have God's Word available to him in his mind for every day of the year. How easy it would have been for him to stop studying what God's Word had to say about fear at 365 days. Surely that would be enough. What were the chances that he would need a verse for leap year too? Yet Richard memorized that last verse—day 366—the exact verse he needed on the day he was taken.

No matter what challenges, hardships, or torment we face in life, we need God's sustaining Word to maintain our walk of faith. Psalm 119:11 makes our need clear: "I have stored up your word in my heart, that I might not sin against you." If we do not know and live by God's Word, we will not face life as God intends.

Refusing to know and live by God's Word has grave consequences. No matter who we are or what we may have accomplished to advance God's kingdom in the world, we need to know the Word, understand it, remember it, and live it out no matter what.

How many "days" of God's Word do you have hidden safely in your heart and mind? What have you tucked away to sustain you when life becomes more difficult than you ever have imagined? Do you know enough of God's Word to rely on for a month? A week? A day?

What are you willing to do to prepare yourself to live out your faith in any circumstance? Will you begin to commit the faith- and life-sustaining Word of God to memory in your mind and heart? Yes, it may take years to study and even memorize everything you need, but you can start today. You can start with just one verse.

Start by memorizing just twelve verses—one for each month of the year. When you have these hidden in your heart, start adding verses—one for each week of the year. You already will have twelve memorized—only forty more to go! If you just do that much, you have acquired a significant arsenal of God's truth and sustaining presence to help you walk out your faith no matter what comes. And you can continue to add verse after verse so you become fully armed for the battles ahead. Will you do it? Here's one way to start:

1. Choose your topic(s). Richard chose fear. You may want to choose verses that focus on God's presence with his people or what God says about worry or anxiety, faithfulness, or love for one's enemies.

2. Choose your verse(s). You may want to begin with verses you are already familiar with. To research unfamiliar verses, use a topical Bible, concordance, or online search.

3. Begin memorizing. Find a way that works for you to keep God's Word constantly in your heart and mind.

# Standing Firm on the Word of God

The law of your mouth is better to me
    than thousands of gold and silver pieces....
Oh how I love your law!
    It is my meditation all the day.
Your commandment makes me wiser than my enemies,
    for it is ever with me.
I have more understanding than all my teachers,
    for your testimonies are my meditation.
I understand more than the aged,
    for I keep your precepts.
I hold back my feet from every evil way,
    in order to keep your word.
I do not turn aside from your rules,
    for you have taught me.
How sweet are your words to my taste,
    sweeter than honey to my mouth!
Through your precepts I get understanding;
    therefore I hate every false way. (Ps. 119:72, 97–104)

5

# THE PASTOR'S WIFE

*The secret police greatly persecuted the Underground Church,
because they recognized in it the only effective resistance left.
It was just the kind of resistance (a spiritual resistance) that,
if left unhindered, would undermine their atheistic power.
They recognized, as only the devil can, an immediate threat to
them. They knew that if a man believed in Christ, he would
never be a mindless, willing subject. They knew they could
imprison the physical body, but they couldn't imprison a man's
spirit—his faith in God. And so they fought very hard.*

Richard Wurmbrand, *Tortured for Christ*

# Session Start-Up

## Let's Talk about That One

What did Richard recognize about the reason behind the intense persecution he and others involved with the underground church suffered under the Communist regime in Romania and its secret police?

What insight does this give us into the nature of the spiritual battle that we, as followers of Jesus today, are engaged in against Satan?

How aware are we that our Enemy is potent, active, and fighting very hard against us?

Why is loving God and seeking to love others as he commands such a great threat to Satan's agenda?

When the Enemy fights very hard against us, what must we do if we want to survive, overcome the opposition, and advance God's kingdom?

## Let's Pray Together

*Dear Lord, it is easy for us to be lured into living a comfortable life, unaware of the reality of the spiritual battle being waged against us and your kingdom. Rather than fighting the Enemy to advance your kingdom and claim the victory, we sometimes distance ourselves from the consequences of living out our faith, seek safety in isolation, or deceive ourselves into believing that what we could do would not have much impact. Forgive us, Lord for our complacency and lack of faith in you. We thank you for the life testimonies of Richard and Sabina who understood the importance and intensity of the battle and responded to it so faithfully and fearlessly. Teach us to walk with our eyes wide open, searching for every opportunity to take up the fight and share your love with people who need a relationship with you. In the strength of your wisdom and almighty power, may we be eager to respond—whether the opportunities seem large or small—and fight to advance your kingdom. We boldly ask this in the name of Jesus, who turned death on the cross into eternal victory. Amen.*

# Video Exploration

## Video Notes

- Take the fight to the Enemy
- Serve the Soviets or go to jail
- Consequences for being a Christian
- Persecuted but not abandoned

- With the Lord we are fearless and strong to advance his kingdom
- In any circumstance we are victorious with God
- We can't make disciples if we don't go
- The price we pay is part of the eternal victory
- Passive perseverance versus faith in action

## Video Discussion

1. Like her husband, Sabina Wurmbrand had a compelling calling to share the love of Christ with everyone she could. Even the dire consequences that likely would come because of political circumstances could not stop her. The situation was so perilous that no matter what she did to live out her faith convictions, there could be no doubt that she was taking the fight to the Enemy. In the scenes of Sabina in the labor camp, what indications did you see of her sense of meaningful purpose, peace, and joy as she lived out her faith under what for many would have been nothing more than disheartening, depressing circumstances?

2. What did you think when you realized the risks Sabina took in order to share just a few words of encouragement from God's Word with other prisoners?

Sabina could have taken a passive and presumably safer course during her imprisonment. She didn't have to share Bible verses with others. She could have reacted very differently when the guards threw her into the river. What do you think inspires some followers of Jesus to reject a passive perseverance and go on the offensive, actively living out their faith no matter what the consequences?

When we think of going on the offensive and living out our faith without reservation, we often think of doing something big that gets a lot of attention. Sabina's efforts to advance God's kingdom weren't like that. Instead, she offered continual expressions of God's love and faithfulness to people in every circumstance she could.

Did her "small" acts require any less courage or faithfulness to be a witness for God than if she had done something "big"? Why or why not?

Were her "small" acts any less of a victory for advancing God's kingdom? Explain.

Sabina also never stopped picking away at the Enemy. One conversation at a time, one phrase from the Bible shared over and over, one person touched by the love of God—she never let the Enemy rest. What can we learn from her example about how to faithfully advance God's kingdom no matter how dire or hopeless our circumstances may be?

3. As you mentally review the scene of Sabina's middle-of-the-night arrest—a situation played out in other homes many thousands of times during the years of persecution in Romania—what do you think was different about the way she responded compared to how others may have responded?

Discuss the many ways Sabina boldly lived out her faith even during those stressful, life-changing moments. Consider, for example, her comment about the "arms" in her house, the impact her prayer had on everyone (secret police included) in the room, and her last words encouraging her son to stay strong in his faith.

4. What do you think Cole Richards meant when he said we are always victorious when we act intentionally on God's behalf?

What makes us victorious even when we pay a price for our faithfulness?

# Growing into a More Biblical Faith Perspective

## Our Study Together

Four years into his second imprisonment, Richard became terribly ill and was moved to a prison hospital. One day he and the other patients were ordered to march into the courtyard and participate in a makeshift theatrical performance, the point of which was to mock Christianity. One by one the prisoners were forced to take center stage and repeat blasphemous slogans against Christ. "We *have* to say these things until it's over," one of the prisoners said, clutching Richard with tears in his eyes.

When it was Richard's turn, he remembered Sabina's words at the Congress of the Cults: "Wash this shame from the face of Christ." He began cautiously, "It's Sunday morning, and our wives and mothers and children are praying for us, in church or at home.

We should have liked to pray for them too. Instead we've watched this play."

Richard saw tears running down faces as he spoke about families. "Many here have spoken against Jesus," he continued, "but what is it that you actually have against him? You talk about the proletariat, but wasn't Jesus a carpenter? You say that he who doesn't work shall not eat, but this was said long ago in Paul's second epistle to the Thessalonians (2 Thess. 3:10). You speak against the wealthy, but Jesus drove the moneylenders from the temple with whips" (John 2:14–15).

The commandant scowled but listened, hoping Richard would say enough to warrant execution. "You want Communism," Richard continued, "but don't forget that the first Christians lived in a community, sharing all they had (Acts 2:44). You wish to raise up the poor, but the Magnificat, Mary's song at Jesus's birth, says that God will exalt the poor above the rich" (Luke 1:52–53).

Richard went on to quote Karl Marx who wrote that Christianity is the most fitting form of religion. Then Richard began to preach openly about Jesus, what he accomplished on the cross and how much he loved even the Communists—especially the Communists. Richard could have been minutes from his death, but he continued his sermon, telling the entire prison that Jesus gave eternal life to anyone who repented. Before he could finish, the prisoners erupted in cheers.

Richard's bold speech cost him his place in the prison hospital, a flogging he didn't think he would survive, additional intense beatings, and blaring loudspeakers to brainwash him.

But as one of the other prisoners observed, "You've undone all their work!"[1]

A passive faith doesn't invite persecution. Often it is possible to be quiet and to escape undisturbed. But do we really want to rob God's kingdom of a victory like the one Richard won in the prison hospital? Do we want to deny salvation to the lost? Do we want to miss out on the joy of taking up our cross and participating in the eternal victory won for us through the blood of Jesus?

1. Love is the most powerful motivator known to humankind. Other than love for God, his fellow prisoners (believers and unbelievers alike), and even his torturers, what could have motivated Richard Wurmbrand to risk giving the sermon he gave in the prison courtyard? What did Jesus tell his disciples about this kind of love (John 15:13)?

What example of love does Jesus use to describe how much he loves us and how he wants us to love one another (John 15:9–12)?

2. Jesus's sacrificial death on the cross and his resurrection on the third day is not only the ultimate expression of love but also the greatest offensive attack on Satan in history. In what specific

ways did Jesus, the sinless Son of God, respond to the suffering he endured on our behalf (1 Pet. 2:19–24)?

What does his example help us understand about how we are to endure the suffering that is part of the spiritual fight we take on when we choose to live out our faith in bold action?

In what way can the example of Jesus encourage us to endure through whatever opposition we face as we boldly live out our faith (Heb. 12:2–3)?

3. When we accept God's gift of salvation, he calls us to live out our faith in everything we do and say. Putting our faith into action is essential to living a life that pleases God. What picture of how to live out an active faith do we begin to envision from 1 Timothy 6:11–12 and Titus 2:11–14?

In contrast, how does James 2:14–17 describe faith that is not accompanied by action?

4. In Matthew 28:18–20, Jesus gave his disciples—and all who would follow him in the future—the assignment of an active faith, a faith that would take the fight to the heart of the Enemy. What is that fight, and by what power and presence are Jesus's followers able to carry it out?

What do we, as followers of Jesus, become when we accept the commission Jesus has given (2 Cor. 5:20–21)?

Jesus's commission to make disciples requires a faithful and active life of service. What excites you about living the kind of purposeful, blessed, and rewarding life described in the following passages, and why do you think such a life of faith is worth the sacrifices required (Matt. 5:14–16; Rom. 10:13–15; Phil. 3:10–14)?

5. Thankfully, God's power is limitless, and his great love ensures that he will take care of everyone who loves and serves him. What assurance does God's unlimited power combined with his unconditional love provide for everyone who walks with him in faith when we take the fight to the Enemy (Rom. 8:31–34)?

Which two things are we assured of when we face any trouble or persecution in the fight for God's kingdom (Rom. 8:35–39)?

6. Paul's letters to Timothy, his younger brother in faith and ministry, provide essential instruction in faith and encouragement in service to God. At the end of his instructions, what reward did Paul anticipate for himself and for everyone who fights the good fight of faith and finishes well (2 Tim. 4:1–8)?

What victory does a life of active faith—a life lived to love God and one another as he commands—accomplish, and by what power is the victory achieved (1 John 5:1–5)?

## Make It Personal

After Richard was ransomed from Romania and lived in the West, he continued to live out his faith in love, faithfulness, and action as he had chosen to do in his homeland. Although he was physically removed from his prison experiences, he never forgot them, nor did he forget those who continued to suffer as he had. "I tremble because of the sufferings of those persecuted in different lands," he wrote. "I tremble thinking about the eternal destiny of their torturers. I tremble for Western Christians who don't help their persecuted brethren. In the depth of my heart, I would like to keep the beauty of my own vineyard and not be involved in such a huge fight. I would like so much to be somewhere in quietness and rest. But it is not possible."[2]

For Richard, the choice was clear. He simply could not accept a passive perseverance when his love for God and his fellow human beings called for an active faith—a faith that took the fight to the Enemy.

Read Hebrews 10:32–39 and consider how Richard and Sabina's lives demonstrated the active, living faith described in this passage.

Is this the kind of living faith you want to experience? Why or why not?

In the life circumstances you face, what does standing your ground look like?

What suffering, insults, and persecution would you anticipate if you were to engage in the great contest of taking the fight to the Enemy?

In what ways can you stand with your brothers and sisters in Christ who are persecuted and imprisoned for their faith?


What are you willing to lose for the reward God has promised you?


Do you, as Richard did, also feel some desire for a more passive and comfortable faith?


What, then, motivates you to engage in the fight for God's kingdom and not shrink back from the consequences?

## Memorize

And pray in the Spirit on all occasions with all kinds of prayers and requests. With this in mind, be alert and always keep on praying for all the Lord's people. Pray also for me, that whenever I speak, words may be given me so that I will fearlessly make known the mystery of the gospel, for which I am an ambassador in chains. Pray that I may declare it fearlessly, as I should. (Eph. 6:18–20 NIV)

# I Will Take the Next Step

*I can have an active faith that takes the spiritual fight to the Enemy because God is greater.*

No one can say it is impossible to take even one step forward in obedience or service to God. Consider, if you will, the impact of just two steps—one hesitant step taken in the prayer of an atheist Jew, and one pleading promise uttered in the prayer of an old man to meet a Jew and lead him to Christ—that made possible the amazing story of Richard Wurmbrand:

> In an isolated sanatorium, Richard prayed his first hesitant prayer. "God, I'm absolutely sure You don't exist," he whispered. "But if, by some chance, You *do* exist, it isn't *my* job to believe in *You*. It's *Your* job to reveal Yourself to *me*."
>
> As it turned out, Richard wasn't the only man praying to God in the rural hills of Romania. High up in the mountains, in a village as isolated as the sanatorium, an aged German carpenter named Christian Wölfkes had spent the entire night on his knees praying....
>
> "My God," Christian prayed aloud, "I've served You on earth, and I want to have my reward on earth as well as in heaven. And my reward should be that I shouldn't die before I

bring a Jew to Christ, because Jesus was from the Jewish people." He sighed. "But I'm poor, old, and sick. I can't go around and find a Jew. In my village, there aren't any. Bring a Jew into my village, and I'll do my best to lead him to Christ."[3]

We know the rest of the story. Christian Wölfkes found Richard Wurmbrand walking down a street in his village. God had answered his prayer! So Christian took the next step and shared the gospel of Christ with Richard. And the fight to advance the kingdom of God on earth continued in earnest.

What do you learn about living out an active faith that takes the spiritual fight to the Enemy from Luke 10:1–11, 17–24?

How much do you want to live that kind of a rich and meaningful life?

What is your commitment to step forward and boldly express your faith:

- In prayer for the spread of the gospel and for your brothers and sisters in Christ who labor and suffer to make him known?
- By diligently studying the Bible and faithfully sharing its truth and the promise of God's eternal kingdom?
- By boldly expressing God's love for people who do not know him, especially for those who mock your faith or cause harm to the cause of Christ or to those who serve him faithfully?

# Standing Firm on the Word of God

Finally, be strong in the Lord and in the strength of his might. Put on the whole armor of God, that you may be able to stand against the schemes of the devil. For we do not wrestle against flesh and blood, but against the rulers, against the authorities, against the cosmic powers over this present darkness, against the spiritual forces of evil in the heavenly places. Therefore take up the whole armor of God, that you may be able to withstand in the evil day, and having done all, to stand firm. Stand therefore, having fastened on the belt of truth, and having put on the breastplate of righteousness, and, as shoes for your feet, having put on the readiness given by the gospel of peace. In all circumstances take up the shield of faith, with which you can extinguish all the flaming darts of the evil one; and take the helmet of salvation, and the sword of the Spirit, which is the word of God, praying at all times in the Spirit, with all prayer and supplication. To that end, keep alert with all perseverance, making supplication for all the saints, and also for me, that words may be given to me in opening my mouth boldly to proclaim the mystery of the gospel, for which I am an ambassador in chains, that I may declare it boldly, as I ought to speak. (Eph. 6:10–20)

6

# WHERE DID I
# LEAVE OFF?

*Richard raised his voice so other prisoners lying in their bunks could hear. In the dimly lit barracks, all eyes were on the pastor.... During all the years Richard had pastored in Bucharest, he had never experienced the kind of silence that permeated the cell. There were no yawns, no fidgeting, no jokes. Richard looked around the darkening room as he continued preaching about Christ. He saw in his cellmates a congregation he had never known before. Their clothes were soiled, their jaws angled, their cheeks hollow, and their eyes—wide with anticipation—revealed their hunger for the truth Richard was feeding them.*

The Voice of the Martyrs, *Wurmbrand*

# Session Start-Up

## Let's Talk about That One

When our brothers and sisters in Christ are severely persecuted or imprisoned for their faith, how do we expect opposition and difficult, painful circumstances to impact their love for God and the lost and their commitment to walk faithfully with Jesus every day?

What are some of the things we assume people can't do under such difficult circumstances, and what are some of the things they find they can do?

As Richard took in the scene around him, what do you think he realized about his walk of faith and how God might enable him to serve and advance his kingdom, even in prison?

What does this scene help you to realize about the intentionality with which God wants each of us to spend our lives, no matter what circumstances we face?

## Let's Pray Together

*Dear Lord Jesus, we say our deepest desire is to love and serve you, but when our life circumstances become difficult and challenging beyond what we have experienced, we often don't know how to live out our faith for your honor and glory. We struggle to bear the hardships, losses, and pain that taking up our cross and following you requires. The easier path is appealing, and we need your help and presence with us so we may live in a way that counts for your kingdom. Help us to remember what an honor it is to suffer for you as you suffered for us. May our own suffering not blind us to the blessing you intend us to be to our fellow believers and the light you have called us to be to the lost. Help us to keep our eyes fixed on the joy of your salvation and the eternal reward you promise to all who follow you. Guard our hearts from all fear as we seek to live a life worthy of our calling in any circumstance. In the name of Jesus we pray. Amen.*

# Video Exploration

## Video Notes

- Spending our lives in a way that counts
- The honor of suffering for Christ
- We made a deal with the guards: we would preach; they would beat
- Everything we sacrifice for God is worth the joy that fills our hearts

- Gratitude to God in the midst of hardship
- Continuing the work of Christ—together
- God is at work in the midst of the worst possible circumstances
- I'm already sold to a future in heaven
- No need for hate or fear

## Video Discussion

1. All of us are spending our lives. No matter who we are, what our circumstances may be, or what we do, time ticks on and is gone. What kinds of things do we generally think make our lives valuable and worthwhile—make us feel good about ourselves and our role in the world?

To what extent are the things we have identified dependent on "good" circumstances?

To what extent do the things we have identified matter from the perspective of eternity?

Why is it important for followers of Jesus in any life circumstance to pursue lives that are fulfilling, worthwhile, and make a difference in terms of eternity?

2. In what sense was Richard intentionally spending his life for the cause of Christ while he was in prison just as he would have spent it had he not been in prison?

In what way did his responses to his circumstances surprise you?

Which perspectives and attitudes do you think are necessary in order to live faithfully for God as he did, and why?

3. What do you think of the "deal" Richard and his fellow Christians made with their guards: the men would preach, the guards would beat, and everyone was happy?

What was rewarding about that arrangement for the Christian prisoners, and how do you think it was possible to be joyful in the circumstances they faced?

4. We often view sacrifice as being a loss, yet in God's kingdom sacrifice is viewed "as a good trade." What is your understanding and experience of offering a sacrifice to God that in turn fills our hearts with joy?

5. In the scene of the house church gathering, what did the description of church being a *lifestyle*, not a *club*, mean to you?

What did you notice about how important the house church meeting seemed to be to those who were involved?

Do you see contrasts between how you participate in your group or church and the way the Romanian Christians gathered together to worship God and support one another under the constant threat of persecution?

6. When the men in prison were worshipping God and celebrating Communion using whatever scraps of bread and water they had, how important do you think it was to them that they were *together*?

> What role do you think the prayers, love, encouragement, and sacrifice for one another that circulated in that community of believers played in enabling them to not only survive but live lives that counted for eternity in the midst of desperate circumstances?

# Growing into a More Biblical Faith Perspective

## Our Study Together

When we are dedicated to following Jesus with all our heart, mind, and strength, we are spending our lives in a way that counts for eternity. But when the life of love and service we have known is taken away, as it was for Richard and Sabina when they were imprisoned for their faith, how do we still live in a way that counts? Life in prison is so different.

In prison, we can't preach God's Word to our church congregation. *Or can we?* We can't share our meal with our friends in need. *Or can we?* We can't share God's love with the lost. *Or can we?* We can't tend to a sick neighbor. *Or can we?* How the Wurmbrands did these things may have been a bit different when they were persecuted or imprisoned, but opportunities to spend their lives for the benefit of God's kingdom were not lacking.

In light of their experience, what is the key to living a Christian life that counts in any circumstance? Perhaps Richard's experience of rediscovering joy while in solitary confinement will give us a start.

> I found that joy can be acquired like a habit, in the same way as a folded sheet of paper falls naturally into the same fold. "Be joyful," is a command of God. John Wesley used to say that he "was never sad even one quarter of an hour." I cannot say the same of myself, but I learned to rejoice in the worst conditions.
>
> The Communists believe that happiness comes from material satisfaction; but alone in my cell, cold, hungry, and in rags, I danced for joy every night.... Words alone have never been able to say what man feels in the nearness of divinity. Sometimes I was so filled with joy that I felt I would burst if I did not give it expression. I remembered the words of Jesus, "Blessed are you when men come to hate you, when they exclude you from their company and reproach you and

cast out your name as evil on account of the Son of Man. Rejoice in that day and leap for joy!" I told myself, "I've carried out only half this command. I've rejoiced, but that is not enough. Jesus clearly says that we must also leap."

When next the guard peered through the spy-hole, he saw me springing about my cell. His orders must have been to distract anyone who showed signs of breakdown, for he padded off and returned with some food from the staff room: a hunk of bread, some cheese, and sugar. As I took them I remembered how the verse in Luke went on: "Rejoice in that day and leap for joy—for behold your reward is great." It was a very large piece of bread—more than a week's ration.

I rarely allowed a night to pass without dancing, from then on; although I was never paid for it again, I made up songs and sang them softly to myself and danced to my own music. The guards became used to it. I did not break the silence, and they had seen many strange things in these subterranean cells. Friends to whom I spoke later of dancing in prison asked, "What for? What use was it?" It was not something useful. It was a manifestation of joy like the dance of David, a holy sacrifice offered before the altar of the Lord.

I did not mind if my captors thought I was mad,
for I had discovered a beauty in Christ that I had
not known before.[1]

1. Richard chose joy not to make himself feel better, but in order
to obey Jesus's command and live in a way that brought honor to
him. In Luke 6:20–23, what promises did Jesus give to his disciples
prior to his teaching about rejoicing and leaping?

Why do you suppose this passage was on Richard's mind while
he was in solitary confinement, and how might it encourage
him to spend his life on what really mattered in his situation?

What are some of the reasons to choose joy in any circumstance (Ps. 5:11–12; 16:11; 19:8)?

2. In addition to choosing joy in all circumstances, we can also live
with an attitude of gratitude. Which good reasons to be thank-
ful in all circumstances do we find in 1 Thessalonians 5:16–18,
23–24; and 2 Thessalonians 1:3–7? Discuss how important they

are in everyday life as well as when enduring persecution and imprisonment.

3. Even though there is nothing appealing about suffering, many Christians who have endured through suffering consider it to be an honor and joy to suffer for Christ. Take, for example, the suffering Pastor Milan Haimovici willingly endured for others and for the cause of Christ: "The prisons were overcrowded and the guards did not know us by name. They called out for those who had been sentenced to get twenty-five lashes with a whip for having broken some prison rule. Innumerable times, Pastor Haimovici went to get the beating in the place of someone else. By this he won the respect of other prisoners not only for himself, but also for Christ whom he represented."[2]

> Pastor Haimovici was willing to sacrifice his own comfort—and indeed risk his life—in order to bring honor to Christ and perhaps convince some of his fellow prisoners of Christ's love for them. His sacrifice is not unique. Even Paul and Silas suffered in this way with joy. What impact did their suffering have on other prisoners and their jailer (Acts 16:22–34)?

In what ways do these examples of faithfulness rewrite our definition of a fulfilling and joyful life that truly matters?

4. When we feel the pressure of opposition or persecution in our walk with Christ, it is easy to wonder if we've made a mistake, if we really are pleasing God, or if we are making a difference that matters. These doubts can be disheartening and make us question if what we face is even possible to endure. But the Word is sure that whatever we do in faithful obedience to God is pleasing to him and will bear fruit. What can we count on if we faithfully walk with Jesus in any circumstance (1 Cor. 15:57–58; 1 Pet. 1:3–9; Mark 10:27–30)?

5. Fear is a natural human reaction to persecution and the harm and suffering that often comes with it. What is Jesus's answer to our fear (Matt. 10:26–31; 28:20)?

6. Jesus never intended for his followers to serve him alone. Living a life that counts for eternity includes our care and support of one another. This is something we need to learn to do. What practical and meaningful things can we do in our relationships with one

another to encourage and support our work for God's kingdom (Rom. 12:9–13; Eph. 4:1–3; 1 John 3:16–18)?

## Make It Personal

When Richard was released from his long imprisonment, he made his way in prison rags toward home. Strangers, who immediately knew where he had been, talked with him and asked about loved ones he may have encountered or heard about in prison. Knowing he had nothing, they offered fare for the tram and the treat of fresh strawberries. When Richard reached his own front door, he hesitated:

> They were not expecting me, and I was a fearful sight in my filth and rags. Then I opened the door. In the hall were several young people, among them a gawky young man who stared at me and burst out, "Father!"
>
> It was Mihai, my son. He was nine when I left him; now he was eighteen....
>
> I turned to Mihai. Three of our visitors—one a philosophy professor from the university whom I had not met before—had told me that evening that my son had brought them to faith in Christ. And I had feared that, left without father or

mother, he would be lost! I could find no words for my happiness.

Mihai said, "Father, you've gone through so much. I want to know what you've learned from all your sufferings."

I put my arm around him and said, "Mihai, I've nearly forgotten my Bible in all this time. But four things were always in my mind. First, that there is a God. Secondly, Christ is our Savior. Thirdly, there is eternal life. And, fourthly, love is the best of ways."

My son said, "That was all I wanted."[3]

We live an impoverished faith if we are not putting ourselves on the line for Jesus Christ. When father and son met after so many years apart, each was greatly encouraged by the testimony of the other. They each had witnessed for Christ and experienced eternal victory in the midst of their suffering and could rejoice and give thanks that their suffering and labor for the sake of Christ had not been in vain.

In what ways does their example challenge you to live a life of joyful discipleship in any circumstance?

Read Colossians 1:9–14. Are you asking and seeking to be filled with spiritual wisdom and the knowledge of God's will?

What does it mean for you to "walk in a manner worthy of the Lord" (v. 10) in all your circumstances?

Through which good works are you seeking to bear fruit?

In what ways are you increasing in your knowledge of God?

Are you choosing endurance and patience with joy and thanksgiving?

In addition to asking God for all of this for yourself, what commitment will you make to pray the same for your persecuted brothers and sisters in Christ?

## Memorize

> And so, from the day we heard, we have not
> ceased to pray for you, asking that you may be
> filled with the knowledge of his will in all spiri-
> tual wisdom and understanding, so as to walk in a
> manner worthy of the Lord, fully pleasing to him:
> bearing fruit in every good work and increasing
> in the knowledge of God; being strengthened
> with all power, according to his glorious might,
> for all endurance and patience with joy; giving
> thanks to the Father, who has qualified you to
> share in the inheritance of the saints in light. He
> has delivered us from the domain of darkness and
> transferred us to the kingdom of his beloved Son,
> in whom we have redemption, the forgiveness of
> sins. (Col. 1:9–14)

# I Will Take the Next Step

*I can experience a fulfilling life of joyful discipleship in any circumstance.*

Richard Wurmbrand wrote:

> Around me were "Jobs"—some much more
> afflicted than Job had been. But I knew the end
> of Job's story, how he received twice as much as

he had before. I had around me men like Lazarus the beggar, hungry and covered with boils. But I knew that angels would take these men to the bosom of Abraham. I saw them as they will be in the future. I saw in the shabby, dirty, weak martyr near me the splendidly crowned saint of tomorrow.

But looking at men like this—not as they are, but as they will be—I could also see in our persecutors a Saul of Tarsus—a future apostle Paul. And some have already become so. Many officers of the secret police to whom we witnessed became Christians and were happy to later suffer in prison for having found our Christ. Although we were whipped, as Paul was, in our jailers we saw the potential of the jailer in Philippi who became a convert. We dreamed that soon they would ask, "What must I do to be saved?" In those who mocked the Christians who were tied to crosses and smeared with excrement, we saw the crowd of Golgotha who were soon to beat their breasts in fear of having sinned.

It was in prison that we found the hope of salvation for the Communists. It was there that we developed a sense of responsibility toward them. It was in being tortured by them that we learned to love them.[4]

No matter what hardship or persecution we encounter in our walk with God, we are called to live lives that honor him and make a difference for eternity. So what is your next step? What are you willing and honored to spend your life on as part of the community of Jesus followers around the world?

Read 2 Corinthians 1:3–11, which gives us a picture of how all followers of Jesus are bound together in the privilege and joy of supporting one another in the sacrifice of suffering for God's kingdom.

In what ways does this passage encourage you to step out boldly and spend your life on what matters for eternity?

In what ways does it prompt you to take obedient, meaningful action in serving your fellow believers who suffer as they spend their lives on what matters for eternity?

# Standing Firm on the Word of God

What then? Only that in every way, whether in pretense or in truth, Christ is proclaimed, and in that I rejoice.

Yes, and I will rejoice, for I know that through your prayers and the help of the Spirit of Jesus Christ this will turn out for my deliverance, as it is my eager expectation and hope that I will not be at all ashamed, but that with full courage now as always Christ will be honored in my body, whether by life or by death. For to me to live is Christ, and to die is gain. If I am to live in the flesh, that means fruitful labor for me. Yet which I shall choose I cannot tell. I am hard pressed between the two. My desire is to depart and be with Christ, for that is far better. But to remain in the flesh is more necessary on your account. Convinced of this, I know that I will remain and continue with you all, for your progress and joy in the faith, so that in me you may have ample cause to glory in Christ Jesus, because of my coming to you again.

Only let your manner of life be worthy of the gospel of Christ, so that whether I come and see you or am absent, I may hear of you that you are standing firm in one spirit, with one mind striving side by side for the faith of the gospel, and not frightened in anything by your opponents. This is a clear sign to them of their destruction, but of your salvation, and that from God. For it has been granted to you that for the sake of Christ you should not only believe in him but also suffer for his sake, engaged in the same conflict that you saw I had and now hear that I still have. (Phil. 1:18–30)

# How to Pray for the Persecuted Church

- Pray for persecuted believers to sense God's presence (Heb. 13:5).
- Pray they will feel connected to the greater body of Christ (1 Cor. 12:20, 26).
- Pray they will be comforted by God when their family members are killed, injured, or imprisoned for their witness (2 Cor. 1:3–5).
- Pray they will have more opportunities to share the gospel (Col. 4:3).
- Pray for the boldness to make Christ known (Phil. 1:14).
- Pray they will forgive and love their persecutors (Matt. 5:44).
- Pray their ministry activities will remain undetected by authorities or others who wish to silence them (Acts 9:20–25).
- Pray they will rejoice in suffering (Acts 5:41).

- Pray they will be refreshed through God's Word and grow in their faith (Eph. 6:17).
- Pray they will be strengthened through the prayers of fellow believers (Jude 20–25).

# NOTES

## Session 1

1. Richard Wurmbrand, *The Oracles of God* (Bartlesville, OK: Living Sacrifice Book Co., 2006), 74.

2. The Voice of the Martyrs, *Wurmbrand: Tortured for Christ—The Complete Story* (Colorado Springs: David C Cook, 2018), 107.

3. Richard Wurmbrand, *From the Lips of Children: A Delightful Collection of Children's Views of God* (Bartlesville, OK: Living Sacrifice Book Co., 2013), 120.

## Session 2

1. The Voice of the Martyrs, *Wurmbrand: Tortured for Christ—The Complete Story* (Colorado Springs: David C Cook, 2018), 61–62.

2. The Voice of the Martyrs, *Wurmbrand*, 178–79.

3. Richard Wurmbrand, *Tortured for Christ*, 50th ann. ed. (Colorado Springs: David C Cook, 2017), 75, 79.

4. Wurmbrand, *Tortured for Christ*, 85.

5. Richard Wurmbrand, *From the Lips of Children: A Delightful Collection of Children's Views of God* (Bartlesville, OK: Living Sacrifice Book Co., 2013), 119.

# Session 3

1. The Voice of the Martyrs, *Wurmbrand: Tortured for Christ—The Complete Story* (Colorado Springs: David C Cook, 2018), 313.

2. The Voice of the Martyrs, *Wurmbrand*, 270–71, 273.

3. Sabina Wurmbrand, *The Pastor's Wife: A Courageous Testimony of Persecution and Imprisonment in Communist Romania* (Bartlesville, OK: Living Sacrifice Book Co., 2005), 183.

4. Richard Wurmbrand, *Tortured for Christ*, 50th ann. ed. (Colorado Springs: David C Cook, 2017), 68–69.

5. Richard Wurmbrand, *From the Lips of Children: A Delightful Collection of Children's Views of God* (Bartlesville, OK: Living Sacrifice Book Co., 2013), 117.

# Session 4

1. Sabina Wurmbrand, *The Pastor's Wife: A Courageous Testimony of Persecution and Imprisonment in Communist Romania* (Bartlesville, OK: Living Sacrifice Book Co., 2005), 96–97.

2. The Voice of the Martyrs, *Wurmbrand: Tortured for Christ—The Complete Story* (Colorado Springs: David C Cook, 2018), 182.

3. Richard Wurmbrand, *In God's Underground* (Bartlesville, OK: Living Sacrifice Book Co., 2004), 109–10.

# Session 5

1. The Voice of the Martyrs, *Wurmbrand: Tortured for Christ—The Complete Story* (Colorado Springs: David C Cook, 2018), 343–46.

2. Richard Wurmbrand, *Tortured for Christ*, 50th ann. ed. (Colorado Springs: David C Cook, 2017), 105.

3. The Voice of the Martyrs, *Wurmbrand*, 32–33.

# Session 6

1. Richard Wurmbrand, *In God's Underground* (Bartlesville, OK: Living Sacrifice Book Co., 2004), 56–57.

2. Richard Wurmbrand, *Tortured for Christ*, 50th ann. ed. (Colorado Springs: David C Cook, 2017), 54.

3. Wurmbrand, *In God's Underground*, 187–88.

4. Wurmbrand, *Tortured for Christ*, 78–79.

# ABOUT THE VOICE OF THE MARTYRS

The Voice of the Martyrs (VOM) is a nonprofit, interdenominational Christian missions organization dedicated to serving our persecuted family worldwide through practical and spiritual assistance and leading other members of the body of Christ into fellowship with them. VOM was founded in 1967 by Pastor Richard Wurmbrand, who was imprisoned fourteen years in Communist Romania for his faith in Christ. His wife, Sabina, was imprisoned for three years. In 1965 Richard and his family were ransomed out of Romania and established a global network of missions dedicated to assisting persecuted Christians.

Be inspired by the courageous faith of our persecuted brothers and sisters in Christ and learn ways to serve them by subscribing to VOM's free monthly newsletter. Visit us at persecution.com or call 1-800-747-0085.

Explore VOM's five main purposes and statement of faith at persecution.com/about.

To learn more about VOM's work, please contact us:

| | |
|---|---|
| United States | persecution.com |
| Australia | vom.com.au |
| Belgium | hvk-aem.be |
| Canada | vomcanada.com |
| Czech Republic | hlas-mucedniku.cz |
| Finland | marttyyrienaani.fi |
| Germany | verfolgte-christen.org |
| The Netherlands | sdok.org |
| New Zealand | vom.org.nz |
| South Africa | persecution.co.za |
| South Korea | vomkorea.kr |
| United Kingdom | releaseinternational.org |